BEING

Grateful

A grateful heart is a happy heart!

BEING

Grateful

How to Open the Door to a More Fulfilled & Abundant Life in 13 Easy Steps

Janice Almond

LOS ANGELES   WASHINGTON D.C.

Copyright © 2015 Janice Almond

BEING GRATEFUL: How to Open the Door to a More Fulfilled & Abundant Life in 13 Easy Steps

Published by ZION Publishing House

Los Angeles & Washington D.C.

www.zionpublishinghouse.com

Printed in the United States of America

ISBN 9780692489826

Cover by *Chantal Hayes Designs*

All rights reserved solely by the author. The author guarantees all contents are original and do not infringe upon the legal rights of any other person or work. No part of this book may be reproduced in any form without the permission of the author. The views expressed in this book are not necessarily those of the publisher.

Unless otherwise indicated, Bible quotations are taken from the Holy Bible New King James Version®, copyright © 1982 by Thomas Nelson, Inc. Used by permission. All rights reserved.

Other version used is: *New International Version, (NIV)*. Copyright © by Zondervan Publishing House, 1984. Used by permission. All rights reserved.

FOREWORD

I just finished Janice Almond's new book *Being Grateful: How to Open the Door to a More Fulfilled & Abundant Life in13 Easy Steps*

I am so thankful that I was selected to be one of the first readers. I was drawn to the book by its title. I continued to read it because of its up-lifting content and easy to read format.

The practical lessons and reflective exercises help to develop a grateful heart, one of the key ingredients for a happy, productive, and abundant life. As a pastor, in Janice's book, I now have an effective tool to share with my flock for the developing of a grateful heart and a positive world view.

Janice's book is great food for the soul. In the book, Janice is non-judgmental and transparent with her own struggles to develop an attitude of Being Grateful therefore the book has the feel of authenticity.

Almond draws deeply from her varied life experiences and her illustrations hit home and clarify the principles and benefits of Being Grateful. I highly recommend this book. It is a quick read for our hurried times. I know it will help everyone who reads it, and it will change the lives for good of those who do it.

Great Job! Janice Almond Keep Going.
Professor/Pastor Omar A Muhammad, Th.M.

INTRODUCTION

Come along with me on this journey. It will be a great one. I promise you. Isn't it time for you to really experience life, fully while you can, while you have the chance? As most of us do, we seem to put off living. Why? Why do we seem to always be in limbo, waiting for something or someone to change, get better? It seems as if we can't, we don't, or we won't appreciate the fact that we are alive for only a limited amount of time. Because of our preoccupation with tomorrow, we are neglecting today.

If you have ever felt this way, this book is for you. What I am about to share with you can and will change your life, your way of looking at things, the way you look at life and experience life. Remember, we are one on this human journey, and these thirteen steps are your key to unlock the door to a life of fulfillment and abundance. Take a chance and explore these notions with me. Believe it or not, everyday can be a good day. It all starts with being grateful and having a grateful heart. This may be hard for some, even for you, but it is possible.

Just so you know, I haven't always been grateful or had a grateful heart. As a young wife and mother, ungratefulness, at times, caused me to have a lack of joy and produced a heavy heart. A lack of gratefulness tends to cause not only a heavy heart but also prolonged pain. You may be feeling a heavy heart right now or unbearable pain. Deep down inside I know you want to be free. You want the heaviness lifted. I know I did. It's time to implement a different way of living. Wouldn't you agree?

It may not be easy at first. You may struggle some. But, in the end, I believe you will see this route is the best and only alternative to unlocking the door to your freedom. Making a change is never easy, but if it's for the good, it's usually for the best.

Know this, we are not alone. You are not alone. You can be grateful. You can **B**elieve in yourself, **E**njoy your journey, **I**nvest in yourself, **N**ever give up, **G**row in love, **G**ive to others, **R**eceive from others, **A**lways be positive, **T**urn obstacles around, **E**nvision success, **F**eel fulfilled, **U**nite for the good, and **L**ook to the future. Let's not delay. This is the day to begin.

Let's begin to open the door. Let's find the answer by pursuing these thirteen steps. Let's call them "life-changing attitudes." As we look at these steps, one at a time, you will come to see and recognize your freedom is just around the corner. Just keep walking and pursuing. Whether you are a teenager, a young adult, a parent, a grandparent, a single person, male or female, you can and will succeed by following the steps outlined on this journey.

STEPS:

Foreword v

Introduction vii

   STEPS: ix

STEP #1—Believe in Yourself 1

STEP #2—Enjoy Your Journey 9

STEP #3—Invest in Yourself 19

STEP #4—Never Give Up 25

STEP #5—Grow in Love 31

STEP #6—Give to Others 39

STEP #7—Receive From Others 45

STEP #8—Always be Positive 53

STEP #9—Turn Obstacles Around 61

STEP #10—Envision Success 69

Step #11—Feel Fulfilled 75

STEP #12—Unite for the Good 81

STEP #13—Look to the Future 87

   About the Author 92

   ONE LAST THING 93

STEP #1—BELIEVE IN YOURSELF

"LIFE WILL PAY WHATEVER PRICE YOU ASK OF IT!"

TONY ROBBINS

CHOOSE TO BELIEVE IN YOURSELF. On this journey called "life", if we don't believe in ourselves, there is not much we can do or accomplish with this life we've been given. We will be stuck, immobilized, similar to being connected to a stake in the ground. Believing in ourselves is something we must all do. We must know there is something this current life has to offer us. Where does this belief in ourselves come from? It comes from the value that we place on ourselves and our life. It comes from within.

How do I know this is true? Believe it or not, it basically all boils down to faith. What do you have faith for? What can you believe for? You are on this planet for some reason, right? So, I guess it's time for you to figure out why you're here. If you have little faith, you will have little belief. How do we go about believing in ourselves? I believe it's in the mind. It's a mind game. We must think bigger and ask for more. We have to believe we are worth it.

Let me ask you a question, "How valuable do you see yourself?" The more value you have and feel about yourself, the more you will believe in yourself and what you can do and accomplish. The more you will seek, and the more you will find. Really, it's all in our perception. Our perceptions determine our lives. At a Chinese restaurant recently, I got a fortune cookie. Inside it read, "Attitudes are the forerunners to conditions." What did Henry Ford, the late great auto maker, say, "If you think you can, you can; if you think you can't, you can't, either way, you're right!" This is our first attitude that must change, what we perceive, think, believe, and say about ourselves.

Our conditions, most often than not, are a result of our thoughts and attitudes. Our thoughts take us places we don't always want or desire to go. This is indeed true because two people can be going through the same, let's say, negative situation or environment- one person can still see the light at the end of the tunnel, while the other can only see darkness. You know this is true. We are getting what we are perceiving.

How do you go about believing in yourself? What do you tell yourself? In the book *14,000 Quips and Quotes* by E.C. McKenzie, is this quote: "If your life looks cloudy, maybe the windows of your soul need washing!" How do you clean your soul? By what you believe, which determines what you say and what you do. Believing in yourself is a conscious, active decision. When I taught high school English, I would always tell my students, "Stop telling your brain what you don't want it to believe!" So, my question to you is this, "What are you telling *your* brain?" Whatever it is, your brain is believing it and what you believe, you say! Change your belief by unclouding your mind.

This can become a never-ending cycle. What we believe, we receive because whatever we tell ourselves over and over again, we eventually start to believe it. Then once we believe it, we say it, and act upon it for the good or for the bad. Think about that for a minute. Doesn't that make you stop and pause and wonder about your deep-seated, inner beliefs? Can't you see how your thoughts are keeping you bound or setting you free? What are you thinking and believing about yourself and your life right now at this present moment?

DO NOW: Try this exercise. Grab a sheet of paper and jot down the first three to five things that come to your mind. Are they good things or bad things? Are these thoughts hurting you or helping you? Now, take another minute and reflect on someone who you think has it worse than you. How are you feeling now? What are you believing now? Has your perspective changed?

All you really have to do is change your perception to change your life. Joni Eareckson Tada did just that. Listen to her story, a diving accident in 1967, when she was sixteen, left her paralyzed from the neck down. She could have given up on her life, but she didn't. She learned to paint using her mouth to hold the paint brushes. She started to believe she had a chance and therefore, she took it. You must believe you have a chance and take a risk to fail but to finally succeed.

Today, Joni is an internationally known mouth artist, a talented vocalist, a radio host, an author of seventeen books, a movie has been made about her life, and she has a prison ministry where she speaks to prison inmates and has them construct and repair wheelchairs for the handicapped. What did she choose to believe about herself? What was her perception? Did she focus on what she couldn't do or on what she could do?

How about you? Do you focus on what you can do or on what you can't do? It's been said that what we focus on gets bigger or expands. I suggest we choose to allow our minds more flexibility, more risk-taking, more excellent thoughts. If you can't and don't believe in yourself, you won't have a reason to try anything. Makes sense, doesn't it?

I'm reminded of the song sung by LeeAnn Womack, *I Hope You Dance*. In that song are the lyrics, "When you get the chance to sit it out or dance, I hope you dance." What makes you believe in yourself? What makes *you* dance? Whatever it is will come from deep within, from your soul. Joni could have had the attitude, *"Well, I'm paralyzed. I guess there's nothing to do but sit here and moan."* Joni could have chosen to sit it out, but she chose instead *to dance*. You can choose to sit it out or you can choose to dance.

Not believing in yourself will cause you to miss out on life and waste your life. Truth be told, it will cause you to miss your potential. We all have a lot of potential. There are so many things that we could do, but most of the time, we don't even think about them. We don't even "tap" our potential. If most people believe that we have this one lifetime, why would we waste any of it by not believing in ourselves? If in reality, life is so short, why wouldn't we, as they say, "go for the gusto?"

I'm sure we all know people who seem to be wasting their lives by their non-believing attitudes. People who complain, murmur, gripe, are never happy or content, and put themselves and others down. Having this lack of belief causes a lack of abundance in every area of life. You can't soar with the eagles wallowing around in the mud with the pigs. There is no way to find fulfillment in life without belief.

Keep track of your thoughts. Literally, change the picture that you have of yourself. If your thoughts or pictures are limiting you in any way, change them! On my journey, this is what I've had to do over and over again. Even when circumstances were not good, I focused on things becoming better. You have to decide to do this, too.

We can't receive what we can't or won't believe. As a high school speaker and debater, I always knew, felt, and believed that I would win, come in first place, at every speech contest. I received about 45 trophies proving I was right. What good does it do to not believe in yourself? It does no good at all. Think about the limitations we force upon ourselves by our lack of belief. We keep ourselves frozen, unable to move. You've seen those movies where there is this force field blocking someone's ability to move forward. It's like that. You want to move forward, but you feel stuck, bound. But, you can break through this barrier.

It takes getting in touch with our inner soul to believe in ourselves. We need to change our beliefs. Perhaps you need to window wash your soul. Be bold to ask for more of life. Our ability to have an abundant life depends on it. Overwhelmingly how we act stems from what we deeply believe. Yes, it's that important.

DO NOW: Try another exercise. Take a sheet of paper and number from 1 to 10. At the top of the paper write this statement-

WHY I SHOULD BELIEVE IN MYSELF: list ten reasons. If you can only think of 5, then write 5. Find at least one thing on the list you can be grateful for.

If you are having difficulty coming up with a list, maybe you can't think of reasons to believe in yourself because no one has ever really believed in you. I believe in you. That's why I am taking you on this journey with me.

COMPLETE THIS SENTENCE:

The things that I will do to change my beliefs are…

8 BEING GRATEFUL

STEP #2—Enjoy Your Journey

"Enjoy Yourself.

It's Later Than You Think."

Chinese Proverb

CHOOSE TO ENJOY YOUR JOURNEY. What does that mean? It means to enjoy your life. You may be asking, "How do I do that?" Sometimes this is easier said than done. When you enjoy something, you take pleasure in, have satisfaction, and experience joy. Too many people are not enjoying their lives for one reason or another.

DO NOW: Take this quick test to determine whether or not you are enjoying your journey. As you read the 20 words and phrases below under each category, put a mental check by which phrase most adequately describes you.

10 BEING GRATEFUL

A person who <u>**ENJOYS LIFE:**</u>

sees glass half full

sees a light at the end of the tunnel

sees obstacles as opportunities

is optimistic

is happy

is patient

has joy

has peace

has faith

focuses on solutions

hopes

perseveres

thinks positively

trusts

always sees the good

sees everyday as an adventure

remains calm

has passion

smiles easily

moves forward

A person who
DOESN'T ENJOY LIFE:

sees glass half empty

sees no light at the end of the tunnel

sees obstacles as dead ends

is pessimistic

is unhappy

is impatient

has no joy

has no peace

has no faith

focuses on problems

doubts

gives up

thinks negatively

frets

always sees the bad

sees everyday as a chore

angers easily

is dull

frowns easily

remains stagnant

12 BEING GRATEFUL

How did you do? Do you enjoy life or do you not enjoy life? Maybe sometimes you enjoy life and maybe sometimes you don't?

Here's a point to ponder from thegoodvibe.co: "As you breathe right now, another person takes their last. So stop complaining and learn to live your life with what you have." In other words, quit waiting to enjoy your life. It may be later than you think.

Make a decision right now to have and enjoy life. Make a decision to stay in the ENJOYS LIFE column. Whatever you have to change, change.

How many years do you have left to live? You don't know, do you? Shouldn't that be a reason enough to live your life as fulfilled as you possibly can? We have to stop letting so many weeks and months go by while we mope. Since we have come to realize our thoughts determine the outcomes of our lives, we now commit to control our thoughts.

We commit to stop making excuses for not enjoying our lives. We choose to believe in our unlimited capabilities. We let our imagination run wild. We can enjoy our journey because we are still on it. We can be grateful for that. True, our circumstances are far from perfect, but who ever said we have to have a perfect life before we can enjoy it?

Let me say, if you are waiting for a perfect life before you can enjoy yours, you may be waiting an extremely long time. If you woke up this morning and could see, walk, taste, feel, or hear, you are blessed and have a reason to be thankful. I am assuming you were able to brush your teeth, comb or brush your hair, put on your clothes, drive to work or school or get a ride, and later at nighttime, you were able to have somewhere to lay your tired body. Am I correct?

Enjoying our journey is a choice we all make. Ask yourself, "What excuse or excuses am I making for not enjoying my life?" First of all, you have to know what you want out of life. If you want nothing, that's exactly what you'll get.

DO NOW: Take some time and write or jot down what you want. Brainstorm ideas for your life. What brings you passion? What makes you light up? We all have something. Find a reason to live for. Apathy is easy. Lastly, you have to do more than try to enjoy your life. That usually won't work. You're going to have to actively and purposefully do something different. You're either doing or you're not. You're either finding joy or you're not.

Granted, you may have strong, convincing reasons why it is hard for you to enjoy your life. You, like Joni Eareckson Tada, may be paralyzed. You may not have been able today to dress yourself, brush your teeth, or comb your hair. Perhaps you are unable to drive or hold a job. Maybe you are in constant pain, taking chemo or drugs just to stay alive. Live your life with what you have. Surprisingly enough, someone else has it worse.

You may be asking yourself, "Why should I enjoy my life?" Well, let me ask you something, "Why shouldn't you enjoy your life?" You may think your life is not worth living, but what else are you going to do with it? If we have to live it anyway, we might as well enjoy it. Who knows how much life we have left?

Take an imaginary stroll through the graveyard. What are your thoughts as you meander around? Are you in a hurry, dying to be one of the occupants? Look at the tombstones. See the dash between the two numbered years. (i.e. 1964-2012), what is that dash? That dash was their life. What will you accomplish and experience between that dash? Whose life will you touch? What legacy will you leave?

I came across this quote-unknown: "There are too many people in too many cars in too much of a hurry going too many directions to get nowhere for nothing." How sad. The human rat race. We don't want that to be our epitaph. It is imperative that we appreciate life now. Right now in this moment! Not tomorrow. Tomorrow may never come. It's vitally important to think of the numerous ways we can appreciate the life we've been given. Don't look for a perfect life before you show appreciation for the life that you have. It indeed may be later than we realize.

Going to the mailbox in my neighborhood, I overheard an older gentleman ask a fellow, female neighbor how things were going. Her reply was, "I'm breathing!" I said, "I know that's right!" Just reflect on that. Your breathing is a cause for joy.

In order for us to really enjoy our lives-our journey here on this earth-we have to make the best of it, good and bad. In the *14,000 Quips and Quotes* book is found another proverb-pearl of wisdom-, "You'll have a better life if you make the most of the best and the least of the worst!" I have a couple of friends, Ben and Shari. They are a married couple who have recently been told they both have bone cancer. But even so, they continue to enjoy their journey. They are making the least of the worst. You can do that, too. Whether you realize it or not, this journey we are on, is helping to mold us into the person we were meant to be.

Let's make a new determination to have fun, to see every day as an adventure, and to expect an abundance. What do we have to lose? What might we have to gain? We just need to take one step and then another. We just need to trust the process and relax. Take our lemon-related problems and make some lemonade.

Do this tomorrow. Instead of complaining, when you wake up in the morning, look in the mirror and tell yourself, "Today is a good day. This is a day of victory in my life. I'm expecting favor today!" Tell yourself, you're taking your lemons, struggles, etc., and making lemonade. Believe your life is worth living, and it will be. Don't just make a mad dash to the end. Don't just hurry through, going nowhere and accomplishing nothing.

In the movie, <u>The Bucket List,</u> starring Jack Nicholson and Morgan Freeman, their characters are dying of cancer. They meet in the hospital and shortly thereafter make the decision to not die until they have seen the world, so to speak. Morgan Freeman, Carter, asked Jack Nicholson, Cole, two questions: "Have you found joy in your life?" and "Have you given or brought joy to anyone?"

The theme of the movie is to live and enjoy yourself, accomplish and do what you can, and not give into excuses. Enjoy your life before it's too late. Stop waiting. Start your "bucket list" now. Death is coming for us all. Look for the joy no matter how hidden it may be. And, with everything you can muster, release joy into the atmosphere.

DO NOW: Try another exercise. Take a sheet of paper and number from 1 to 10. At the top of the paper write this statement-

WHY I SHOULD ENJOY MY JOURNEY: and list as many reasons as you can.

COMPLETE THIS SENTENCE:

Things I can do to enjoy my journey are...

18 BEING GRATEFUL

STEP #3—INVEST IN YOURSELF

"DO SOMETHING TODAY

THAT YOUR FUTURE SELF WILL THANK YOU FOR."
www.indulgy.com

C**HOOSE TO INVEST IN YOURSELF**. Why is investing in yourself important? When you invest in yourself, it proves that you love and care for yourself. It's a way of showing gratitude to the One who created you. You have to give time to yourself. Most of us just rush around until we wear ourselves out, never taking time out for ourselves. How long do we really think that is going to work? We already know it is not working. Possibly thousands if not millions are in mental chains, exhausted in body, mind, and spirit, wishing they could be free. True freedom comes from slowing down some. Getting off of the treadmill for a minute.

These lives of ours remind me of a hamster we used to have when our kids were small. The hamster just used to go around and around in this plastic ball. Spinning, spinning, spinning and going nowhere. This is a never-ending cycle, which can't do anything but leave you frustrated, feeling hopeless. We are working so hard, but for what? We are forgetting to dance and thereby neglecting ourselves.

20 BEING GRATEFUL

Look at what is happening because we are not putting ourselves first.

Well-beingindex.com states the reported incidence of diabetes is on the rise in the United States, climbing to 11.3% of American adults -- or about 26 million Americans -- in the third quarter of 2009, up from 10.4% in the first quarter of 2008. If current trends continue, 15% of American adults -- or more than 37 million Americans -- will be living with diabetes by the end of 2015.

The U.S. obesity rate, which has a well-established relationship with diabetes incidence, is up about one percentage point in quarter-over-quarter comparisons with 2008 results. (Obesity is assessed on the basis of respondents' self-reports of their height and weight, which are then used to calculate standard Body Mass Index scores. Individual BMI values of 30 or above are classified as "obese.")

The upward trends in obesity rates almost certainly play a substantive role in the increase in diabetes rates over the same time period. Americans who are obese are nearly three times as likely as those who are not obese to report having been diagnosed with diabetes. More than one-fifth (21.2%) of obese adults are diabetics, compared to 7.4% of non-obese adults."

The above study appeared on gallup.com in an article entitled: "U.S. Diabetes Rate Climbs Above

11%. Could Hit 15% by 2015." The article goes on to say that "one of the best ways to reduce obesity" is by exercising. There were lower incidences of diabetes from those who exercised at least one day a week for at least 30 minutes. Now tell me truly, how really difficult is that to do? You and I both know your life is worth it.

Exercise is one way of investing in yourself. Physical activities, such as, brisk walking, bicycling, and swimming lead to weight loss, lowering of blood pressure, and can reduce insulin dependency, if done along with proper meal planning. Relaxing, resting your mind, and forms of meditation are also ways to invest in yourself.

Why is relaxing and resting your mind so important? Too much stress as we all know can kill us. Stress can cause high blood pressure, heart attacks, and even strokes. I know about this first-hand--the ills of high blood pressure. When I get stressed out, my blood pressure goes sky high. In fact, that is one reason why I no longer teach high school English full-time. We must take care and invest in what is and will ultimately matter the most overall.

About five years ago, I basically passed out while I was teaching. I had to get practically carried to the nurses' office. My blood pressure was taken. The reading was 184/120. That was the day I found out I had high blood pressure. Needless to say, my health is the most important thing I have. We all have to take our health or lack of it seriously. To drive this point home, two of my best friends, who were also high school English teachers, who had high blood pressure, got strokes and died. Their deaths were a wake-up call for me.

You can invest in yourself by doing something you enjoy. It could be a combination of things, (i.e. reading, drawing, singing, yoga) anything to get you to slow down from your fast, hectic schedule. Or just close your eyes and meditate. What I like to do is put on a YouTube channel/easy listening station. Try it.

DO NOW: Stop reading and go to "relax daily" on YouTube. There are a variety of playlists. Pick one you like. In fact, as I am writing this, I am listening and watching. There is an ocean breeze coming across the "channel" through the pictures. Since I live in Arizona, that's what I have to do- pretend I am at the ocean and can feel the ocean breeze. Take time to close your eyes, just listen, and meditate. Take a breather. Better yet, if you can, take a nap. The book and I will be here when you wake up. We've only just begun our journey.

To tell the truth, everything we do or don't do from the food we eat to the books we digest has a daily affect on us. It takes diligence to watch and control our intake of stuff. We need to ask ourselves if what we're doing, whatever it is, is it a good investment or a bad one? We need to think about the return on our investments. Is this double cheeseburger and extra-large French fries going to help me or hurt me in the long run? Is this television program or movie I'm taking two hours to watch going to increase my life for the better, or am I just lazy?

It should be that what we choose to invest time in and on should enhance the quality of our lives not detract from them. When we wake up and realize that what we give to life and expect out of life-our investment- is what we will receive back in return, we will begin to witness and experience a more acceptable, fulfilled life. We will decide to make better choices and think and plan wiser. Words of wisdom are found in the Book of Proverbs. Here's what you can do, make an investment in and for yourself, a commitment to reading one chapter a day. I was once told to read one a day, which is good for 31 days. Doing this is something you can add to your arsenal.

Investing in yourself takes time, especially if you want to see permanent and lasting change. You can't be in a hurry. Anything worth something is time-consuming. No sweat. No glory. Investing in yourself is another step you must take on your pathway to being grateful. What you want to do, you can do if you invest some time doing it. Everything takes a commitment. Being a good spouse takes a commitment. Being a good parent takes a commitment. Being a good employee takes a commitment. Life is an investment-period, point blank!

It seems like this shouldn't be that hard to understand. Not many things come easy. You must work at them. Whatever you invest in is a commitment and takes a commitment. To be a better you, you have to invest in things that make you better. Honestly, if you want a future, you are going to have to do something today to make it happen.

DO NOW: It's time to make another list. Be personal. Think about why you should invest in yourself. Title the list-

WAYS TO INVEST IN MYSELF: Take a few minutes and write whatever comes into your mind. Don't hurry. Take your time. Pause and think about it.

COMPLETE THIS SENTENCE:

Actions l can take to invest in myself are…

STEP #4—NEVER GIVE UP

"IF YOU PERSEVERE,

GOD WILL TAKE CARE OF EVERYTHING ELSE."

DALE BROWN

C **HOOSE TO NEVER GIVE UP**. It's so easy to quit anything. Look at our society. We are quitting marriages by the droves. What is it now? 50% of marriages end in divorce. This is a sad commentary on our nation. But, I am not just focusing on marriages. This is just indicative of a mindset. In other words, if I don't want to continue, I can just quit. There is no perseverance, no persistence, no going through the struggle. This I QUIT mentality covers the whole gambit. We'll quit on friendships, jobs, exercising, losing weight, eating right, making a difference, even writing a book, and the list goes on and on. Why are we as humans so quick to quit, give up, and throw in the towel?

We seem to forget the fact that nothing happens overnight. Everything is a process-a journey. That's what we can't stand and don't like-- the process. We seem to have no patience for the process, the work. We want instant. Instant coffee, instant food, instant love or instant sex, instant happiness, and instant money. Waiting? Persevering? Persisting? They sound like foreign terms to our ears. You have to build the life you want. It takes a diligent effort and time.

For example, according to www.examiner.com, "a study by the Gates Foundation, Public Agenda stated that according to the U. S. Department of Education fewer than 60% of all students who begin higher education at 4-year institutions receive a degree within six years. And these statistics reflect an average—at some institutions, the numbers are truly disturbing." The study goes on to cite various explanations, lack of preparation, lack of skills, lack of money, and lack of interest being some. Although most of the six-hundred respondents, aged 22 to 30, believed that having a college degree paid off, those who quit were "less likely to feel passionately about the value of college." – "Why So Many Students Who Start College Never Finish."

Passion? You hear a lot about that word passion or passionate. You have to have a passion for what you do to continue along a particular course. While, I agree with this to a certain extent, in some ways, I disagree. In some ways and incidences, passion can be fleeting. Being married, as I have, to the same man for almost forty years, it is not always an everyday passionate experience. Sometimes it takes more than passion. You have to be determined. It takes commitment. In fact, all of these thirteen steps are commitments. LIFE takes a commitment.

To have the mindset of never giving up, one has to value something. Life in general, has to be valued. How much do you value your life? What is it that you want to contribute to society? Contemplate the answers to these questions to give you the fortitude to persevere. You should know that you can't accomplish anything or even attempt to have an abundant life if you are always giving up.

What happened to, I WILL-UNTIL? I remember seeing a poster of a frog's head inside of a duck's mouth and the frog is holding onto the duck's neck. The caption reads: Never Give Up!

We need a new mentality. A never quit attitude, even if we fail. Failure is not the end of the world. The late Zig Ziglar, a motivational speaker and writer of thirty-three books, once said, "Failure is a detour, not a dead-end street." In fact, as long as you're alive, you can make a U-turn, an about-face. Just don't quit. Or, just start again or find another way. Fail your way to the top! All it really takes to accomplish our goals, dreams, and desires is diligence, not perfection. Who cares if you're not the best? Perfection doesn't reside in humans, anyway. Perfection is not the answer, never giving up is.

Think back in your life to when you've had to persevere through an issue or a challenge. How did it make you feel when you could look back after you were on the other side of that event? You most likely felt some sense of relief and accomplishment, right? You felt a sense of fulfillment. This reminds me of a time when, as a high schooler, I was one of the ones selected by the principal to travel for the summer to Europe as a part of an organization called, People to People.

People to People made all of the travel arrangements, hotel lodgings, food, etc., but each individual student had to raise his or her own funds. This was a challenge for me. I wasn't really sure even where to begin to start raising money. Needless to say, one of the other students who was also going, came up with a brilliant idea. Being in a rural area, there were lots of farms around. We-a group of about seven of us-decided to go around and ask the farmers to donate produce, vegetables, etc. that we could sell at the school.

Not only did we sell vegetables, but we also conducted other means of raising the money we needed. We held car washes, bake sales, sold dinner plates, etc. I got numerous babysitting jobs and saved my money from being an aide at a board and care facility directly across the street from the high school. Also, because there were articles in the city's newspaper about our endeavor and planned trip, we all received various monetary donations. It seemed like an insurmountable hurdle for some of us, but we persevered. We made it happen.

That is what never giving up can do. Never giving up will allow you to become a stronger person. Without a doubt, you will grow from the experience. You can make something happen in your life if you make quitting not an option. Just go through what you have to go through. It's very easy to look at some circumstances as not being pleasurable or desirable, but even during these times, grit and determination can save the day. Simply, get back up when you fall down.

Harriet Beecher Stowe, American abolitionist and the author of Uncle Tom's Cabin, a novel which depicts the way life was for African-Americans during slavery, once stated, "When you get into a tight place and everything goes against you til it seems you cannot hold on a minute longer, never give up then for that is just the place and time the tide will turn." Just persevere and trust in God. Let Him take care of what you can't.

Everybody has issues, challenges. Instead of giving up, HOPE UP! Look for a message you can hear or a lesson you can learn and take it to heart. Grab some trust and faith. In reality, you are essentially no different from any other person on this planet. Since you are here living on this earth, existing in human flesh, you can finish what your

30 BEING GRATEFUL

Creator has begun. Say, "I will finish!" "I WILL FINISH!"

DO NOW: Another exercise. Use a sheet of paper to number from 1 to 10. At the top of the paper write this statement-

WHY I SHOULD NEVER GIVE UP: and list up to ten reasons. I hope you are beginning to realize your "why" is more important than the "do." Let me share a secret with you, if you have no why, you will have no do.

COMPLETE THIS SENTENCE:

I will never give up by …

STEP #5—GROW IN LOVE

"YOU CAN'T TRULY LIVE IF YOU DON'T TRULY LOVE."

JANICE ALMOND

C**HOOSE TO GROW IN LOVE**. Do you really want an abundant life? Do you want a life filled with joy and happiness and fulfillment? It takes growing in love. Love is the answer. This is an important step because without love, our lives have no meaning. You know that, and I know that. 1 John 4:8 says, "... for God is love." You can't influence anyone or anything without love. The driving principle is love. St. Augustine, an early Christian theologian once said, "He who is filled with love is filled with God Himself."

A friend of mine, in his sixties, who is waiting for a heart transplant said to me the other day, "Why didn't I love enough?" He has had heart issues for over ten years, wasn't taking care of himself, exercising, or eating right. While visiting him in the hospital, he also mentioned about how he has come to realize it's all about relationships and started admonishing me and others, by way of texting, to show love to others; in other words, make sure other people, your family and friends know that you love them, now. He said, "Don't wait to love."

32 BEING GRATEFUL

This is indeed an excellent warning for everyone on this planet. One we need to adhere to.

Listen to the words of this song by Diana Ross and Diane Warren:

"Sometimes we search this world for gold. When all we really need is just a hand to hold. Sometimes we let the greatest treasure just slip away with words we forget to say, too many times, but always after all, Love is all that matters."

Today and every day in the future, make a commitment to grow in love. As in most things, sometimes we need to just take baby steps toward achieving a goal. So, we will let love be our goal. We will tell if we are progressing in love by how well we treat others. We will ask ourselves, how patient are we? How kind are we? How gentle are we? Are we choosing to exhibit a loving heart even when others are unloving? Can we truly turn the other cheek? If we can't, and we don't, we might as well say goodbye to the human race. Somebody has to choose love. So many people on this planet think it is money we need, but it is love we need.

Every time you help someone less fortunate than you that is love. Every time you go above and beyond your duty that is love. Every time you turn the other cheek that is love. Every time you do what is good that is love. Every time you choose love over hate that is good.

Dr. Martin Luther King, Jr., the late civil rights leader of the 60's, once said, "Hate cannot drive out hate, only love can do that." Look at all the racial tension and hatred we are experiencing in this country today. Martin Luther King, Jr. must be rolling over in his grave. We haven't progressed much, have we? Where is the love? When are we going to finally experience what he dreamed? In his "I Have a Dream" speech, from the steps of the Lincoln Memorial in Washington, D C, on August 28, 1963, he talked about freedom and justice for blacks. He talked about rising from the …. "valley of segregation" to the sunlight of "racial justice."

In addressing the mostly black audience, Dr. King went on to say, "Let us not seek to satisfy our thirst for freedom by drinking from the cup of bitterness and hatred…We must not allow our creative protest to degenerate into physical violence…We must rise to the majestic heights of meeting physical force with soul force…We cannot walk alone." This last phrase was also directed to the whites in the crowd of approximately 250,000 marchers.

Today, we are still enduring racial injustice. Today, we are still not experiencing brotherhood. Today, we are still seeing hatred and brutality. Today, we are still witnessing physical violence. Today, we are still not equal. Our only hope is love. We are all Americans. One day we must come to realize this and embrace our commonness. We focus too much on what separates us. Love unites. Hatred divides. Love is life. Hatred is death.

While writing this book, a very good high school friend of mine died. He was a cheerleader with me in high school. At his passing, there were many accolades about the love he showed to all. Incidents such as these make me ponder about what will be said of me upon my death. We can all hope that we will be remembered for our love. The Bible states in Proverbs 10:12, "Hatred stirs up strife, but love covers all sins." Everyone has wronged someone else. In a manner of speaking, we are not to be concerned with whether we receive love but only that we give it. It's not "I love you if you love me;" it's "I love you," period.

It's important to grow in love because love is freeing. Our daily actions prove whether we are truly free or if we're bound. We have the keys to our freedom. Don't hold grudges. Just let bygones be bygones. We can all do it. We can allow this head knowledge to become
heart knowledge. We can move past logic to emotion. When will we as Dr. Martin Luther King, Jr. wanted, hold hands? When will we be free?

Think of some ways you can grow in love. Determine from this moment on to make a real difference in the lives that you come into contact with every day. One thing I have decided to do is pray with and for more people on a daily basis. I have been pleasantly surprised. Most people, after sharing with me some issue they're facing or going through, desire prayer right then and there. Recently, I was talking with an elderly lady in the library who has congenital heart failure. She was thankful for the prayer. I find prayer is uplifting to myself and others and is a way to show and give love.

What are some ways you can show and demonstrate love? Jot down a few... taking time to listen to someone in pain, preparing a meal for someone who is sick, getting someone out of their house or apartment who is unable to drive, being patient and kind to others, and just being available to help or assist someone less fortunate than you. I'm sure you can think of more. Think outside of the box and take action!

Mainly, we just need to be more open to opportunities as they present themselves. One opportunity I presently have is going into a prison in Arizona to teach, preach, and pray for the men imprisoned there. In leading a class in how to experience God, I am noticing my love is growing for these men. I find myself praying for them now on a daily basis, even as I am away from them.

The interesting thing about praying for others is your love grows for those you are praying for. That's why the scriptures say, "...pray for those who spitefully use you and persecute you," in Matthew 5:44. You can't hate someone you're praying for.

DO NOW: Try this exercise. Stop reading and close your eyes. Say a short prayer for someone who you are having ill feelings toward. Keep doing this on a daily basis. You will notice yourself starting to feel amiable toward this person. I have tried this numerous times myself. It never fails.

How do you really grow in love? The answer lies in walking in forgiveness. Forgiving and forgetting. Refuse to hang onto anything and everything and anyone and everyone who or that has hurt you. This is tough. We all know this from experience. But, we also know that it is tougher to hang onto the pain. Holding onto the pain keeps us in bondage and unable to love. Love is grace in action. We say, "Yeah you deserve it, but you get a PASS!" This is another choice we must make. To truly live, you must truly love.

Do this exercise. Take a sheet of paper and number from 1 to 10. At the top of the paper write this statement-

WHY I SHOULD GROW IN LOVE: and list five to ten reasons. The more reasons you can list, the better. This will prove to yourself that you have deep, sincere motivations for having and living a more fulfilled, growing in love, life.

COMPLETE THIS SENTENCE:

Actions I can take to grow in love are…

38 BEING GRATEFUL

STEP #6—GIVE TO OTHERS

"YOU HAVE NOT LIVED A PERFECT DAY

UNTIL YOU'VE DONE SOMETHING

FOR SOMEBODY WHO CANNOT REPAY YOU."

JOHN WOODEN

CHOOSE TO GIVE TO OTHERS. How much of a giving person are you? Or, are you a giving person? The answer to these two questions has a lot to do with the quality of your life. Stinginess doesn't bring much fulfillment. And let me ask you another question, would you rather be around a giving person or a selfish person? Most people would rather be around a giving person.

How do you become a giver? It's another choice, another commitment. A giving person sees outward/outside themselves. A true, giving person thinks of others first. A stingy, selfish person only sees toward themselves-what someone might call, "naval gazing." This type of person only looks and only cares about what concerns them, their needs. He or she is so busy staring at their own belly button, they can't see and don't focus on anyone or anything else. We all have gone through this at one time or another, and we all know someone like this.

40 BEING GRATEFUL

There is an old saying, "It is more blessed to give than to receive," which is actually, Acts 20:35. Just for this one reason, you should be a giver. Why? To be blessed! To be blessed means enjoying happiness; bringing pleasure, contentment, or good fortune. Giving to others can and will bring you happiness and contentment; whereas focusing only on yourself and your issues will in the long run just bring you more pain and cause a more ungrateful heart. Maybe you have experienced this, too. The more you see inward, if you are not careful, the more discontent you can become. Most people would choose to be blessed.

We all remember Mother Teresa. Why? We all remember her because she was a giver. In 1979, she won the Nobel Peace Prize for her work in the struggle to overcome poverty and distress. For over forty-five years she ministered to the poor, sick, orphaned, and dying in Calcutta, India. She felt her mission was to care for all those who felt unwanted, unloved, and uncared for. She once said, "I'm not a social worker. I don't do it for this reason. I do it for Christ. I do it for the church!" When asked what we can do to promote world peace, she said, "Go home and love your family."

Can you imagine how great it would be if everyone you met on a daily basis was a giver? Can you imagine what a difference it would make in our nation, our world? We would indeed have a more peaceful world. Everyone would benefit. It starts with us. Most of the time, as you give, you receive. "Give, and it will be given to you....," Luke 6:38. Be other-centered, not self-centered. Don't be concerned with being repaid.

As a little girl growing up and even as I was older over the years, I witnessed my mom and dad always thinking and caring for other people before themselves. I remember them giving away tons of furniture, etc. whenever we moved. They even practically gave away a couple of cars. My sense of generosity comes from them. Ask yourself if you truly help people.

Surprisingly enough giving can be a little thing. You don't have to give the shirt off your back. You can give a smile. Give a wave. Give a handshake. Give a hug. Here's a quote, "Life is like a mirror. If we frown at it—it frowns back. If we smile—it returns the greeting." from *14,000 Quips & Quotes*, a book mentioned earlier. Just smile at someone today or smile at everyone your path crosses today. Guess what? Most likely, your smile will be returned. Believe it or not, this little, simple thing will bring joy to your spirit and will most likely lift the spirits of the receiver as well.

John Wooden, who was once the championship winning basketball coach at UCLA, was a giver. He is known for saying, "make each day your masterpiece." I read this quote in a book by Pat

Williams, called *Coach Wooden- The 7 Principles That Shaped His Life and Will Change Yours.* How great it would be if we all lived this way. If we gave not expecting anything in return. I knew Coach Wooden when I was a college student at UCLA, from 1971- 1975. While attending there, I was the Bruin Bear female mascot, Josephine Bruin. One of the great things about being the mascot was that I got to travel around the country with the basketball team, even flying on the same plane and staying in the same hotel.

John Wooden was always polite, always calm, always smiling, and always had a kind word to say to us- the cheer squad. It was great for me to be a small part of his legacy.

When Wooden died in 2010, according to a CNN article dated June 4, 2010, UCLA Chancellor Gene Block said of him, "Coach Wooden's legacy transcends athletics; what he did was produce leaders...." And the UCLA Director of Athletics, Dan Guerrero, said, "There will never be another John Wooden...."

What masterpiece are you creating today? What do you plan to do for someone today who can't and doesn't have the means to pay you back? Giving to others is a gift you give to the world whose dividends keep on giving. These dividends keep on going, even after you're gone, departed from this life. Who would not want a legacy like that? Let me share a secret with you. You will be remembered for something. The life you are living right now is speaking volumes. After you die, it's over. When you are gone, people will remember you either as a giver or as a taker. How do you want others to remember you?

Truth be told, you will feel more fulfilled being a giving person. Just serve more. Just give of yourself more. Your life will feel more abundant and more alive. You in turn will be given and receive more. The rest of Luke's verse 6:38 goes on to say, "...good measure, pressed down, shaken together, and running over will be put into your bosom. For with the same measure that you use, it will be measured back to you."

So, in other words, you are receiving what you're giving. Have you pondered that lately? This applies to the good and the bad. Take time today and every day to be mindful and conscientious of what you're "giving." In other words, choose to live a "perfect day" today.

Exercise. **DO NOW**: Get a sheet of paper and number from 1 to 10. At the top of the paper write this statement-

WHY I SHOULD GIVE TO OTHERS: and list up to ten reasons.

44 BEING GRATEFUL

COMPLETE THIS SENTENCE:

Things I can do to give to others...

STEP #7—RECEIVE FROM OTHERS

"ACCEPTING ANOTHER PERSON'S GIFT IS ALLOWING HIM TO EXPRESS HIS FEELINGS FOR YOU."

ALEXANDER MCCALL SMITH

C**HOOSE TO RECEIVE FROM OTHERS**. How do you receive from others? Although it is more blessed to give than to receive, we need to be good receivers as well. Why, you ask? Well, the obvious reason is that a giver needs someone to give to, and for another, you don't want to stop or cut off the blessing of the giver, right? Giving and receiving is a reciprocal process. Let's suppose that you wave at a friend and they don't wave back. That's an example of you giving but them not receiving. Maybe, they didn't see you waving at them. Maybe they thought you were waving at someone else. I'm sure this has happened to every one of us.

Another example might be putting out your hand to shake someone else's hand, but they don't want to reciprocate, don't take your hand. Or, you wanting to give someone a hug, but when you go to do so, they tense up or turn away. Truth be told, when I was mad at my husband, I would do that- tense up or turn away. But, how does this make the other person feel, the one who wants to give? Most likely, the rejected person feels a myriad of emotions- rejection, a sense of loss, misunderstanding, and unappreciation, just to name a few. When people give, they want you to receive.

Believe it or not, just the simple act of listening can be a form of receiving from others. How many people do you know who complain that people don't "give them the time of day?" (don't listen to them). Most people are so frantic with life just trying to "bring home the bacon", they can't be bothered with you and your little, inconsequential issues. We have to start caring more about our neighbors- worldwide. When are we going to truly stop the endless merry-go-round we are on? Choose to listen to someone today and help give them a sense of fulfillment.

Everybody knows a little encouragement can go an awfully long way. You probably need some today. Receive it from me and from others. Don't you know that you can turn your thoughts around just by encouraging yourself? You have this ability inside you. It may sound crazy, but you can receive from yourself. It's the enemy of our souls who is a master at discouragement. Ignore him. "Resist the devil and he will flee from you." James 4:7. This takes practice but begin now.

Until recently, it was hard for me to receive help from people. I have always had the attitude that

I can do it myself. After all, I'm a "Leo!" Now, I don't really follow zodiac signs, but I do take "charge" and am independent. I'm a survivor. Even in my marriage, just ask my husband, David. I'd rather do things myself than ask for his help. This is pride at its worse. Sad to say, this is not a good quality to have. I wasn't letting him express his feelings for me. This attitude only pushes people away and can be the culprit for creating more distance emotionally. Being able to receive from others proves you are humble.

What if I were to tell you, being unable to receive from others is a form of selfishness. It shows you are ungrateful. Notice how children are? Do they have a problem with receiving? No, they don't, usually. Children are, for the most part, eager and anxious to receive. Why? Children believe receiving is a good thing and will be good for them. They expect to receive a benefit from receiving. They don't usually question the motives of the giver. We, as adults are different. We, on the other hand, have a tendency to doubt, question, and second-guess the motives of others. Why?

Every one of us has gone through hurtful experiences which have left us wounded, unable to freely receive. This is a battle we must all overcome to some degree or another. For a long time, it was hard for me to truly believe and receive from white people. Growing up in Sioux City, Iowa, during the fifties, was a hard time for blacks. At that time, we were called negroes. I remember days when, while walking home from elementary school as a kindergartener and first-grader, groups of white kids would throw rocks at me. I had to run just to get away from them.

I know it is hard and painful to break out of habits such as this, and you might be feeling anger, sadness, or even depression. But, let me share a secret with you, as you are able to start to receive from others, you will notice and feel a freeing in and of your spirit. Over time, your heaviness and rejection will depart. Receiving from others is part of what we must learn to do as a part of humanity. It was during my sixth-grade year that I began to open up to a white, male teacher, named Mr. Spiller. I received his gift of learning, of his belief in me. Receiving from him, in the classroom, was akin to a butterfly awakening out of a cocoon. It freed me. Receiving is freeing.

Some don't want to admit it, but we are all in the same boat traveling this road together. This journey will be easier for us all if we can learn to be receivers. The next time someone wants to offer you something; whether a wave, a smile, a handshake, or a hug, freely receive it and freely give back. By doing this, you will help to ensure that person receives their blessing. Did you ever stop to think about that? You must realize you hold the keys to someone else's sense of feeling fulfilled simply by receiving what they're giving, if what they are giving is a good thing, of course.

No matter how hard it may be for you to receive from others, take a leap of faith, and do it for a day. If you can't receive from someone, a family member or a friend because they hurt you, release them by forgiving them. You will both be set free. Isn't that really what you want, freedom? Freedom to be able to truly give and receive? This can only be a reality if you allow yourself to receive from people and let them express their feelings for you. We have to stop being selfish, vindictive, and ungrateful. We have to stop blocking the blessings of others.

It is our option. We get to choose our attitude. It is my belief that learning to receive from others is a gift that you give yourself. After, my sixth-grade year, I started to soar! Starting in junior high school, as it was called then, I began to try my wings, and guess what? They worked! I joined the choir and the orchestra, playing the violin. I became a cheerleader and an A student. I began to love literature and even my white English teacher, Ms. Love. I learned to let go. I learned to be able to attend schools with whites and not let it hinder me from learning. I let the hurtful, mean words bounce right off of me because I now felt worthy. I wonder where Ms. Love and Mr. Spiller are today? What a gift they were to me.

In fact, throughout the rest of my years of schooling, I was almost always the only black in a sea of white. And I became ok with that. I didn't let it stop me. By learning and deciding to change my attitude, my life became richer, more fulfilling, and yours can, too. I was a skinny, pigeon-toed, knock-kneed little Negro girl who was made fun of and called "nigger," more times than I want to remember.

I know you have also had discouragement and disappointment. Many of us have lived our lives believing that people have ulterior motives for what and when they give. But, we don't have to let these thoughts and feelings control us. As we learn to become better recipients, we in turn will become better givers. It is indeed a two-way street.

Although, we don't always want to believe or admit this, we are all inter-connected, regardless of race, religion, or creed. I need you. You need me. We can and must join hands and walk together. Receiving is a way for us to have abundance and live a full life.

DO NOW: Take a sheet of paper and number from 1 to 10. At the top of the paper write this statement-

WHY I SHOULD RECEIVE FROM OTHERS: and list up to ten reasons.

RECEIVE FROM OTHERS 51

COMPLETE THIS SENTENCE:

I will receive from others by...

52 BEING GRATEFUL

STEP #8—ALWAYS BE POSITIVE

"THINK POSITIVE BECAUSE THOUGHTS ARE LIKE THE STEERING WHEEL

THAT MOVES OUR LIFE IN THE RIGHT DIRECTION."

SUGANTHI

CHOOSE TO ALWAYS BE POSITIVE. Why? It is very, very easy to be negative. Negativity just seems to come more naturally. To tell you the truth, it will be hard for us to accomplish any of the steps to being and having a grateful life if we cannot think or be positive. We won't be able to believe in ourselves unless we are positive. We won't be able to enjoy our journey if we are not positive. We won't invest in ourselves because we'll say, "What's the use?" We will give up easily if we are not positive. We won't be able to grow in love or even maintain love if we can't be positive.

Needless to say, giving and receiving will also be a challenge without a positive attitude. For instance, when we give, we may think people will misconstrue our motives and when people want to give to us, we may question their motives. Being and having a negative mindset, can and will only cause us, in the long run, more harm than good. We won't be able to or even feel like turning our obstacles around. We won't be able to envision success. We will feel no fulfillment, won't unite for the good, or look to the future. So, if we know all this, that having a negative attitude is bad for us, what keeps some of us in a negative mindset?

Believe it or not, some of us may not actually know why. Or, we may know why but believe there is nothing we can do about it. That's just how we are. Our family is negative, so we're negative. Well, wake up and make a change today! Acknowledge and recognize this trait in yourself and change it. The late, great Jim Rohn, motivational speaker, once said, "If you don't like where you are in life, change it-you're not a tree." Think of some things you can do and some actions you can take to change your attitude from negative to positive.

One thing you have to do is combat negativity with positivity. Think of or imagine if you will, two boxers in a boxing ring. One boxer is named Negativity and the other boxer is named Positivity. The bell sounds, and they both approach the middle of the ring. The boxer who wins is going to be the one who has the persistence and dedication to overcome.

You must allow Positivity to take more blows and still come out the winner! Negativity is a powerful foe but can and must be defeated. Just ask yourself how bad do you really have it? Could you have it worse? Do you really have NO blessings to count? Remember Eeyore? Eeyore is the character in the Winnie-the-Pooh children's series books by A. A. Milne. Eeyore is mostly always unhappy, pessimistic, skeptical, and believes the worst will happen. He even, ironically, appears to enjoy his personality. He used to say, "It's gonna be another rainy day." He'd do it without even looking for the clouds!

We must fight, "tooth and nail" for Positivity to win.

As a Bible class instructor at a prison in Arizona, I see approximately twenty-five male inmates on a weekly basis. These men, dressed in orange, could have many reasons to complain and some of them do complain, mainly about the food, but in more ways than not, they are a positive bunch. Always joyful to see me, they greet me with a jovial, "Hi, Mrs. Almond!" During the class sessions, we have many opportunities for great times of discussion. One man will pipe up and say something like, "Our bunks are too close together, but I will say God's Word out loud even if I have to whisper." How amazing is that? How would you fare in the prison system?

Truth be told, you are in a prison of sorts if negativity is your main mode of living and being. In fact, I think we all know constant negativity is a drain on our brain. Everybody knows it can be hard being around constantly negative people. Eventually, they can even rub off on us. Being around them and listening to their spiel can have an adverse affect on our minds.

Reading good books, listening to good music, and speaking edifying words can all contribute and have a lasting effect. In Pat William's book, *Coach Wooden- 7 Principles That Shaped His Life and Will Change Yours*, comes an idea that can lead you to a more positive, abundant life, and it's simple. Here it is, "Books are our friends- and our best friend of all is the Bible. In its pages, we find not only insight and knowledge, but also comfort for the soul. Throughout your life, in the good times and the hard times, heed the counsel of Joshua Hugh Wooden: Drink deeply from good books, especially the Bible." For those of you who don't know, Joshua Hugh was Coach John Wooden's father.

What is your choice in music? I am convinced some people don't realize that certain music is not edifying for them. In other words, it's not building them up or benefitting them. For instance, if you just broke up with your significant other, I don't think it's probably a good idea to listen to "Achy, Breaky, Heart." Will that help you or hurt you? We have to be convinced that there is a war going on every second of every day for our mind and what we are thinking. Music is a part of that battle causing us to believe rightly or wrongly, positively or negatively.

Another thing I'm convinced people don't realize is the power of spoken words, the spoken word. So much if not all of what we experience is driven by us. How are we going to possibly live an abundant life if we are always being and saying something not edifying or lifting us or others up? It makes an abundant life virtually impossible because we are repelling it by our actions. We choose to put down and keep down.

Think about it. How different would our society, our lives be if we would remember to be courteous and kind versus mean and fearful and spiteful? These attitudes start in the heart. They start with a positive outlook. Remember, you ARE NOT a tree. You can move and evolve. You can become better. We allow negativity to grab ahold of us. We give it more ammunition than positivity.

It's up to you now. Do you want to break free from negativity and start developing a more positive mindset? Then do that. Heed the suggestions above. There is an old saying, "garbage in, garbage out." What you put in your thinking, stays in your thinking, and manifests outward. Get rid of the stinking thinking.

You need, "positive in, positive out." Everything you input delivers results and determines the output. Start reading good books. Start reading something that uplifts your spirit. Listen to edifying music, speak edifying words, and refuse to allow anything emotionally damaging to enter your soul. Pay attention to the movies you watch. Don't spend so much time dwelling and reflecting on the news of the day. It's not only time-consuming but also energy-draining. The news makes the most of the worst.

We need to counteract the negative news which bombards us all on a daily basis and take control of what we allow in our two ears and between them. Seeing and hearing is oftentimes, believing. This is why we must be the guardians over our mind, spirit, and soul. We have to be diligent in this and keep watch. Imagine a world where positivity ruled? Choose to start moving your life in the right direction. Choose to steer your wheel toward the positive side.

Our positive thinking or negative thinking will drive us either to swim or to sink. We can't brush this off and say what we think doesn't matter. What we think does matter. Proverbs 23:7 states that "As a man thinks in his heart, so is he." This is a strong statement, I know. Haven't we all heard the phrase, "The truth will set you free?" I'm not trying to preach at you, but did you know that that statement also comes from the scriptures and is found in John 8:32? This journey is about freedom and truth. Your abundant life lies just over the horizon. The door is beginning to open.

Most people would agree that being positive and having a positive outlook creates more happiness in their lives. Surprisingly enough, the happier a person is the more fulfilled they generally are. In a book by Dr. Robert Emmons, professor of psychology at the University of California, Davis, *Thanks! How the New Science of Gratitude Can Make You Happier*, on research involving thousands of people conducted by a number of different researchers around the world, studies show that practicing gratitude can increase happiness levels by around 25%.

Emmons research indicated that gratitude can improve your health, relationships, academics, energy levels, and dealing with tragedy and crisis.

The simple act of thinking positive and not complaining will grant you a more fulfilled and abundant life. You can still steer your life in the right direction and be happy. Listen to this quote by Anne Frank, the young, Jewish girl who was a victim of the German Holocaust. She wrote a book entitled, *The Diary of a Young Girl*, which was published in 1947. She wrote, "Whoever is happy will make others, happy, too." "Hurt people, hurt people."

DO NOW: Time to get another sheet of paper and number from 1 to 10. At the top of the paper write this statement-

WHY I SHOULD ALWAYS BE POSITIVE: and list up to ten reasons. As you are doing these exercises, I would suggest that as you think of additional reasons for this step or the previous steps, you simply add them to your list. Keep your notes in a binder or type them up on your note pad on your phone or tablet, etc. and refer to them on a daily basis. Remember, you are retraining your mind and changing your life.

COMPLETE THIS SENTENCE:

Actions I can take to always be positive are…

STEP #9—TURN OBSTACLES AROUND

"DON'T BE AFRAID TO START OVER.

IT'S A NEW CHANCE TO REBUILD WHAT YOU REALLY WANT."

ZIG ZIGLAR

CHOOSE TO TURN OBSTACLES AROUND. Everyone has obstacles. They're a part of life. We have all gone through obstacles and will continue to go through them. Will there ever be a time when you won't have an obstacle? I guess the answer to that is when you're dead.

DO NOW: Take a moment and think of the greatest obstacle that you are facing right now. How can you turn that obstacle around? Think about it for a minute. While you're thinking about it, jot down some ways that you can overcome it. It's easy for us to think we are the only one wrestling with an issue but usually that is not the case. You are not the only one dealing with what you're dealing with.

You might be feeling anger, hatred, frustration, etc. Believe me, I don't like it either, having to deal with obstacles. I know it is hard, painful, and challenging at times. We all have to deal with obstacles. But, our life journey demands it. Hear this statement from Moliere, the 17th century French playwright and actor, "The greater the obstacle, the more glory in overcoming it." Sounds bizarre, doesn't it? Obstacles have to be overcome. Think of a hurdler. He only succeeds by jumping over the hurdle. You will only succeed by facing the obstacle not running from it.

Ok, then. So, what's the answer to you and me overcoming our obstacles? Are you ready for this?

GRIN and BEAR IT! Have you ever seen or read the syndicated cartoon with that name? This feature cartoon is still distributed today. Well, if you want to improve your life, have more joy, and less anxiety, you cannot run from obstacles. You have to continue to smile through the process. You have to deal with the pain in order to get the gain. No pain. No glory. Keep your chin up and keep plugging along. Allow your test to become your testimony. Sometimes this is easier said than done.

Everyone goes through challenges. What is life without a challenge? A challenge brings out the best or worst in us. It shows us our true perspective. It shows us whether we really have the guts to persist in our purpose. I saw this poster once. Most of the poster had a huge mountain and inside the middle of the mountain was an opening. It showed a bird flying toward it. A caption read: "Obstacles are what you see when you take your eyes off your goal."

We have to resolve to keep our eyes on the prize. Whatever it is you are attempting to do, establish, or complete must be tackled head on. Remember, you have greatness to gain. Focus on the answer to the problem. Focus on what you can do, what you can change.

This is what I did when I noticed I had gained forty pounds in one year. I thought to myself, how did this happen? Being a high school English teacher is hard work and not for the faint of heart. During that particular school year, I had been running out of energy. By the afternoon, around 5th period, my batteries were starting to run low. I had to do something quickly. There is no way that you can teach a class full of squiggly ninth graders, if you can barely concentrate yourself. Something had to be done. I thought about "Monster" or "Red Bull" but decided against it. The energy drink, PowerAde came to my rescue.

I was in heaven! I got back on top of my game. No fatigue. No zoning out. No losing focus. In my fifties, I still had it. The students commented, "Man, Mrs. Almond, you have so much energy!" Yeah, I wasn't going to let a bunch of teenagers get the best of me. But, all of a sudden, I began to notice I was gaining weight, lots of it. It was getting so bad, I could barely fit into my pants. I began asking myself, "What's going on?" For the life of me, I couldn't figure it out.

One day in the teacher's break room during lunch, some of us got into a discussion about sugar and sugar grams. To me, this was fascinating because I never remember ever paying attention to health conversations like that before. One teacher, whose classroom was right next to mine, was losing weight. We all noticed it. Her secret? *The Belly Fat Cure* book, by Jorge Cruise. I was more than curious. How could the amount of sugar grams cause weight gain? I didn't get it. I decided to buy the book myself.

Guess what I found out? According to this book, you are only supposed to have a total of 15 grams of sugar a day. I also discovered that sugar turns into fat in your body. So, you guessed what was making me fat? The PowerAde was. I was drinking at least one every day and sometimes two. Here's the kicker. PowerAde, the regular one not the diet one, contains 14 grams of sugar. Just by me drinking one a day, that was already my allotment of sugar for the day. Drinking two should have been a no-no. Then what about all the other foods that contain sugar such as, fruit, juice, vegetables, sauces, BBQ, sandwiches, and even fast food?

My solution was to stop drinking PowerAde. I also started using the "belly fat cure" myself. I lost the weight in 3 months. I am now back in my size 8 jeans. I had been all the way up to a size 12. I know you may be thinking, that's not much of an obstacle. Well, it was to me. I turned this obstacle around.

Surprisingly enough, if you want to overcome and be an overcomer, you have to be able to turn your obstacles around and not allow bad times to overwhelm you. Find a way out or through or around or over. You have to give attention and effort. Find a way to begin again. You have to believe everything will be ok. When you have a rough day or a rough week, tell yourself, "Things will be better tomorrow!" Tell yourself, "I'm going to learn something from this and turn this obstacle around." "I'm fearless!"

No matter what your obstacle is or how painful or distressing it is; whether a health issue, a weight issue, a financial issue, a job issue, or a family issue- there is a way out, around, or through. How, you ask? One way is by remembering there are more people like you who are facing the same issue or an obstacle and are going through it somehow. If plan A, plan B, and plan C have failed, work on plan D. Never forget, the harder the path, the greater the joy.

For one of my personal obstacles, I have joined and reached out to a couple of support groups which have proven to be very helpful and instrumental along my particular journey. I would suggest you get a support group, as well, if you need one. Remember, time is not up to construct the life you can imagine. Give life time to work things out in your favor. A good adage is this- "The harder you fall, the higher you bounce," spoken by Horace, the Poet. When you fall, just bounce back up.

Another way is to keep a good outlook and be patient. Good things come to those who wait and trust. Our next step is to "envision success." Keeping a good outlook goes back to our previous step of always being positive. So much of what we experience in life depends on our attitude about it. It's not so much about what is happening to us as it is to what our reaction to it is. We can change our attitude and change our life. It still comes down to a decision we make, a choice of how we look at things. You can start over. You can have another chance.

There is a story of a prisoner who was describing what he could see out of his prison cell window. He proceeded to tell of how he could see the blue sky, the birds flying, and feel the sun beating down upon him. It was only later after the prisoner was removed from the cell that it was determined that when looking out of the window, there was no sight to be seen, but only a brick wall.

How can you turn your obstacles around? How can you build the life you really want? Start by changing how you "see" things.

Dale Brown, the one-time basketball coach at Louisiana State University, once said, "If you only see the hurdles, you'll never win the race."

WHY SHOULD I TURN MY OBSTACLES AROUND?
Make a list. Do your best to come up with at least five reasons. **DO it NOW**.

COMPLETE THIS SENTENCE:

How I can turn my obstacles around is…

68 BEING GRATEFUL

STEP #10—ENVISION SUCCESS

"MOST MEN FAIL NOT BECAUSE THEY AIM TOO HIGH

BUT BECAUSE THEY AIM AT NOTHING."

AUTHOR UNKNOWN

C**HOOSE TO ENVISION SUCCESS.** Your life can't go according to plan if you have no plan. Having an attitude of success is crucial and vitally important for progress. Whatever you foresee or have in sight can ultimately be obtained. How does this work? It's our focus that drives us toward what we desire. I heard someone say once that what you focus on expands. What are you looking at and what are you expecting? Are you even expecting anything?

In reality, people on the whole, fail to realize and captivate on their full potential. We often fail to adequately recognize our own unique, individual gifts. These failures, along with hesitancy, often stop us in our tracks. Any doubt, and we're out! What would envisioning success look like to you? Just think, what would we really do and accomplish if we had expectancy, a knowing that victory is ours? What would we aim for?

Ask yourself, what is it you feel you can do and want to do? Now, don't compare yourself with anyone else or talk yourself out of going for what you want. What if you could compose the next hit song, pen the next bestseller novel, or invent the next technological breakthrough? Well, you know how all of this can come about? Imagination. Get in a quiet place and meditate. What is the first thing that pops into your mind? Have you ever thought about making a collage of ideas? I am talking about a "vision board."

If you have never heard about this concept, grab a piece of cardstock or a poster size board and let yourself imagine what you could do, where you could go, and who you could become. Let your imagination as they say, "run wild." I created my vision or "dream" board in 2010. At that time, I was teaching high school English. This dream board project was initiated by the school's student council for the entire school population to participate in, this included the teachers.

On my vision board, which was a poster board size, I decided to put my high school senior picture in the very middle. I then put various names around my picture: POET, WRITER, SPEAKER, and SINGER. To the left of the names, I added pictures of places to travel to. I cut out a picture of a woman who looked as if she were leaping for joy and placed that on the bottom right of the poster. Above my senior picture, I have the words, The Power of Walking With God. At the very top of the poster board, somewhat centered, is the phrase: Never Give Up On Your Dreams. Last, but not least, I placed various words and phrases to fill up the entire poster; (i. e.) *You Are Powerful*, *Visionary Leader*, *Education*, *Oh, Yes, I Can*, and *The World Is Waiting-Get Out There And Explore It.*

Surprisingly, since then I have written poetry, become a non-fiction writer, a speaker with "Toastmasters", and have been asked to sing at various community events. It does work! This poster is located on my bedroom wall directly across from my bed where I can constantly view it and read it. I would suggest you make it a priority this week to begin yours. Paul J. Meyer, one of the nation's most inspirational and motivational leaders once said, "Whatever you vividly imagine, ardently desire, sincerely believe, and enthusiastically act upon must inevitably come to pass." This is what a vision board does. It helps you to vividly imagine that what you see and meditate on can come to pass.

Success is hard and takes effort. Anything done well takes work and a lack of sleep! My many years teaching English made that very clear to me. I didn't stand for mediocrity in myself or my students and neither should you. After all, what real enjoyment or pleasure will you get from being just average? Probably, not much.

There you have it. Now, you can finally stop procrastinating. You can finally stop making excuses and blaming every Tom, Dick, and Harry for where your life is right now. I dare you to find something you ardently desire and start today to act enthusiastically upon it. Don't worry. Don't fear. I heard it said fear = false evidence appearing real or forget everything and run! How about we view fear as "FACE EVERYTHING AND RISE!" I heard this statement somewhere and like it. That's a better, more productive way of looking at fear, isn't it?

Make a commitment with me that starting tomorrow morning when you wake up, you are going to look in the mirror and tell yourself, saying OUTLOUD, "Today is a good day. I will have victory today. I'm expecting success today!" Do this every day. Just this one little exercise will do wonders for you. Your mind will be renewed, and you will feel invigorated. What you believe, you can achieve. Don't settle for less. Aim high.

Think about it. If you don't envision or visualize success, what are you going to envision? Failure? How is that going to make you feel, visualizing failure? Not very well, I surmise. You have to know what you want out of life in order to go for it and get it. Being vague is not going to work. Uncertainty and indecisiveness will have us stuck. Going for nothing will get you nothing. Go for your success. You don't have to see the whole path to start walking.

Envisioning success will give you the fortitude to keep pressing on when you feel like giving up. We are not failures just because we have failed. We may have lost some dreams along the way and had some hopes die, but we can learn from the mistakes we made and begin again. That's the beauty of it all.

There is a poem entitled: "Motto for Success" that I used to have my high school English students recite at the beginning of every class. The last stanza reads as follows:

Life's battles don't always go to the stronger or faster man,

But sooner or later the person who wins is the person who thinks he can.

You have to think success, to get success. Thinking failure will only get you more of it. If you can see yourself as successful, you have the ability to be successful.

DO NOW: Take a sheet of paper and number from 1 to 10. At the top of the paper write this statement-

WHY I SHOULD ENVISION SUCCESS: list up to ten reasons.

74 BEING GRATEFUL

COMPLETE THIS SENTENCE:

Things I can do to envision success are...

Step #11—Feel Fulfilled

"You Have Everything You Need

for Complete Peace and Total Happiness Right Now."

Wayne W. Dyer

C**HOOSE TO FEEL FULFILLED**. How do you feel right now, at this current moment? You must have wanted to feel AND be more grateful, or you wouldn't have bought this book. Do you need a reason to feel or be more grateful, more fulfilled? Check your heart. Is it still beating? There's your reason right there. Truth be told, that's really the only reason you need. Everybody knows or at least they should know that feelings are fickle. What you are feeling is most likely what you are getting.

Feelings can at one moment be good and at another moment, be bad. Feelings, as well as thoughts, have to be managed because thoughts create feelings. Good thoughts lead to good feelings. Bad thoughts lead to bad feelings. Feelings of fulfillment have to be chosen. We may not automatically wake up every day and feel abundantly fulfilled. You know as they say, "It's a process!"

76 BEING GRATEFUL

What if you could wake up every day and feel all of the superlatives and blessings of life? Wouldn't you think that that would be the way to live? Believe it or not, waking up is a blessing. The best way to feel fulfilled is to change our attitude about it. We need to make a determined decision to have

"Gratitude with Attitude"

"It's something you choose to think, have, be, and do.

It's something deep inside of you.

It's something you have with you each day.

Something no one can take away.

Your attitude to enjoy life or not

Your attitude to rise or rot

Your attitude to sink or swim

Your attitude- it's much more than a whim.

Today-you choose.

Today-you decide.

Which path you follow

Which horse you ride

Which tune you sing

Which rhythm you dance

Today-your choice.

Today-your chance.

Which game you play

And not delay.

Choose not tomorrow

Choose today

Your attitude."

Can you imagine how great it would feel if starting right now we all would change our attitudes for the better? Think about what great burdens would be lifted. Amazingly, the act of feeling fulfilled, would uplift us all. It would be easier to give a smile if we felt fulfilled ourselves. Everything would be easier.

I'm talking about a light-hearted heart. It takes reaching up and beyond yourself. Or, perhaps going deep inside your soul. Find your "happy place." Just take a minute and go back in your life to when you were a child, to a time when you were innocent, before the craziness started to develop in your life. When you were light-hearted. Meditate on that time, that place, those situations. Smile to yourself as you remember. Imagine what it would feel like to have that feeling of fulfillment return.

I know we all have problems, issues, and challenges. This is the point where we choose to focus on what we have not on what we don't have. In fact, if I just stopped and reflected on the problems I have right now, I couldn't finish this book. I am writing to myself as well as to all of you. We have the option to feel fulfilled and to believe we have whatever we need for peace and happiness.

Learning to feel fulfilled is a great achievement. It is something we have to do on a daily basis. It's not magic. It's a choice. Open your mouth and tell yourself, "I make a choice to feel fulfilled today." A key is never to say or tell yourself, "I don't feel fulfilled." Are you starting to get it now that you are the one running your life by your attitude, thoughts, and words?

Have you ever read James 3:6? It says, "And the tongue is a fire, a world of iniquity. The tongue is so set among our members that it defiles the whole body and sets on fire the course of nature, and it is set on fire by hell." Later on in that chapter it goes on to say that the tongue is used by us to bless and curse others, which ought not to be. But, we are to be peacemakers. We have to take control.

What is happening here is that our tongues with the words that are coming out of our mouths are causing life or death to us and others. The words we speak lead to our fulfillment or unfulfillment. Without really thinking about it, our whole being becomes defiled or corrupted simply by our choice of words. Proverbs 18:21 says, "Death and life are in the power of the tongue, and those who love it will eat its fruit." Pretty scary, isn't it?

You may have not really seriously thought about it, but our lives are set on a course which is for the most part determined by how we talk. This is not advantageous for you, especially if you have had a habit of just allowing any old thing you feel like saying to come out of your mouth. Death or Life? What are you choosing by what you're saying?

We can stop the downward spiral this minute. We are in charge, not our tongues. Today- this is our chance to choose a right and proper attitude.

So, what are some ways you can feel fulfilled? Why should you feel fulfilled?

80 BEING GRATEFUL

DO NOW: Make two lists:

LIST #1 Some Ways to feel fulfilled:

LIST #2 Why I should feel fulfilled

STEP #12—UNITE FOR THE GOOD

"DO NOT BE SIMPLY GOOD-

BE GOOD FOR SOMETHING."

AUTHOR UNKNOWN

C**HOOSE TO UNITE FOR THE GOOD.** United we stand. Divided we fall. This goes for everything, our families, our jobs, our friends, our cities, and our nation. Look how divided our country is right now. We haven't progressed much since the beginning of our nation. In some ways, it seems as if we've regressed. It's hard to agree on almost anything. Where are the moral absolutes? We need some more spiritual warriors. We need workable policies that will bring our world together not continue to tear it apart. We need to unite for the common good.

How do we do this when we have so many conflicting ideas and beliefs? The only thing I really know to do is to pray. Jeremiah 29:11 states, "For I know the thoughts that I think toward you, says the Lord, thoughts of peace and not of evil, to give you a future and a hope." Even with conflicting values, we can come together and unite; in fact, it is imperative that we do or what future will we have?

Ask yourself, what you can do to be a part of the solution and not a part of the problem. Here is a perfect example of becoming a part of the answer: www.gofundme.com. On this website, which is free to sign up, you can make personal pleas for fellow friends, family, or acquaintances. Money is raised on the website with donations from others. Donations are requested for a myriad of situations; cancer victims, burn victims, attack victims, accident victims, all types of family tragedies, to save animals, to save businesses, etc., and the list goes on and on. "Saving Eliza" posted by her parents, raised $1,837,550 to help get four-year-old, Eliza, a life-saving therapy trial for a terminal disease.

This is one way to unite for the good. What are other ways? In our city, once every Wednesday, the pastors of the community come together to pray for each other, the various congregations, and our tri-state community. This is creating a bond between the ministers and the churches, a working together, not a pulling apart.

Also, think of all the community groups, organizations, and clubs that come together on a weekly basis, such as, the Kiwanis, Elks, Lions, Rotary, etc., to discuss and formulate ways to help and give back to their cities and towns. Let's also not forget about the black fraternities and sororities that give back, groups such as, Omega Psi Phi and Delta Sigma Theta. Why do people join such groups?

To give back and feel more abundant, right? To feel like they are doing something to help others is a sense of altruism. It helps us feel more fulfilled. Uniting for the good makes us less selfish. It takes our eyes off of ourselves and onto the well-being and welfare of others. Helping others makes you more grateful and appreciative for what you have.

We see church groups and some religious organizations providing food pantries, shelters, clothing donations, monetary gifts, and more, all to aid our fellow man. Caring about others is the most effective way to have a happy life, even while dealing with problems of our own. Think about it truthfully, for a moment. Don't you feel better when you can help someone in their time of need? I know I do.

Truthfully speaking, as human beings we want to feel and be connected to one another. That's why we have Facebook and Twitter, Google Plus and Instagram, Pinterest and LinkedIn. How many of you have found long, lost friends from many moons ago by checking in and registering on these and other social networking sites? We long to be a part of a larger community. While writing this book, I have had a few people contact me on Facebook, asking me, "Are you Janice Hayes?" Hayes was my maiden name.

Sadly, there is plenty that pulls us apart. Some things are race, gender, religion, money, social status, etc., just to name a few. Look at all the wars. What causes war? Differences. Dwelling on our differences will only keep us apart; whereas, uniting for the good will give us a sense of fulfillment because no man is an island. A contemporary gospel song by Russ Taff goes like this, "You're my brother. You're my sister. So, take me by the hand. Together, we will work until He comes. There's no foe that can defeat us when we're walking side by side. As long as there is love, we will stand."

Let's face it. We all need each other even though we act as though we don't. Democrats need the Republicans and vice versa. We need the Independents, the Tea-Partiers, and the Libertarians. We won't ever accomplish anything worthwhile or lasting without unity. Divided, we cannot stand or create anything good for ourselves, our families, our nation, or this world. Join with me in doing your best to look for the good and promote the good. We should all have a conscience. Working together is the answer.

Resist the urge to throw up your hands and say, "It's no use!" Don't throw in the towel. Someone needs you to be strong and hold on, if just for their sakes. That's what we can all tell ourselves. Can we just hold on for one more second, one more minute, one more hour, one more day, one more week? It doesn't have to be some great, earth-shattering thing that you do. Start small. Reach out to a neighbor.

Together, we are stronger. We can face obstacles better together. We can run races faster together. We can spur one another on toward the future. The late president, Franklin Roosevelt, once said, "People acting together as a group can accomplish things which no individual acting alone could ever hope to bring about." Imagine the strides we can make if we set aside our differences. Of course, we will not always agree; in most cases, we won't agree. This is where agreeing to disagree comes in. But, ultimately, we must look to and for the greater good. Let's work on what we can to bring wholeness to our lives and to the lives of others.

As an African-American woman on my life journey, I see many things terribly wrong in and with our society and often wonder if the chasms can be mended. There are many issues that divide us. This book is not for discussing those issues. Our attention is to be on what brings and causes life not on what brings and causes death.

As my thoughts and our journey are coming to an end, this is a time for us to reflect. We cannot keep running around in circles, going nowhere, caring about only ourselves and no one else. Selfishness is a detriment to our way of life. As you're thinking, remember those in the past and present who have mattered the most to you. More than likely, he or she was a person who gave of themselves, above and beyond what was necessary.

I am putting out a challenge! A CALL to ARMS! Rise up with me, and let's be the people we were created and called to be. Choose to be better, believe stronger, and fight longer- "Reach out and touch somebody's hand. Make this world a better place, if you can!" (song lyrics) written by Nickolas Ashford and Valerie Simpson.

WHY I NEED TO UNITE FOR THE GOOD: List five to ten reasons. **DO it NOW**.

COMPLETE THIS SENTENCE:

Things that I can do to unite for the good …

STEP #13—LOOK TO THE FUTURE

"FAITH GIVES US THE COURAGE TO FACE

THE PRESENT WITH CONFIDENCE AND THE FUTURE WITH EXPECTANCY."

AUTHOR UNKNOWN

FINALLY, **CHOOSE TO LOOK TO THE FUTURE**. This makes sense, doesn't it? Then why do so many of us stress out and continue to stew over the past? It is hard to think abundantly while mesmerized with the past, past victories, past mistakes, past issues, etc. Here's a phrase to adhere to-"Get over it!" Get over the past and press toward the future. We are told to do that in the Bible.

What is so important about looking to the future? If we can't see forward, we can't go forward. The scriptures say, "Where there is no revelation, the people cast off restraint..." Proverbs 29:18. The things that we all do and the actions we take mainly happen as a result of us looking forward toward a goal or some sort of achievement. This is what pushes us forward. This is what enables us to live with hope. We must have faith in the future to go toward it. FAITH, what is that? It's a knowing, a believing that without seeing the evidence, you believe and expect good things to come to pass. Hebrews 11:1 says this, "Now, faith is confidence in what we hope for and assurance about what we do not see."

Let's suppose you had no vision for your future. If this were true, you probably wouldn't even get up out of bed in the morning. If you had no goals whatsoever, why would you even get up? You could just sleep all day. Am I right? You would have no purpose. Something has to drive you, compel you to move. Having no vision for the future-instead of bringing a fulfilled life, brings a depressed life. We have all gone through a time or two of depression, of some kind or another, and pressing forward is the key to freedom. Just practice putting one foot in front of the other, right then left, right then left again.

Malcolm X, the late Muslim freedom fighter for equal rights for African-Americans, mentioned that the future belongs to those who prepared for it. This is precisely why we have to look confidently ahead believing that sooner or later we can and will overcome. What we do today, now, is preparation for our future, our dreams.

I know it can sometimes be hard and painful. But one day you will look back and see just how far you have come. Focusing on the pain of our past is a continual downer. Believe me; I know from experience what a prison this can be. As my husband, a prison chaplain, likes to say, "We are all inmates." We can all be in our own prisons of our own making. We can lose faith.

On a daily basis, we choose either to press forward or to focus on where we currently are. We may not like our living condition, our job environment, or our family situation, but even in the most horrific times, we can fix our minds on some good that will eventually come out of it if we only keep the right focus. Train your mind to have an expectancy of hope and good will.

Looking ahead to the future takes faith, faith in a new and brighter tomorrow. Just because our lives are not perfect is no reason not to look ahead. I have news for you; our lives will never be perfect. There will always be something going on. I heard it once said, "We are either going into a storm, coming out of a storm, or are already in a storm." I would say that pretty much sums it up. We can and should always expect something to be going on. That's called LIFE… accept it gratefully!

Listen to Philippians 3:13-14. "But one thing I do: Forgetting what is behind and straining toward what is ahead, I press on toward the goal to win the prize…" With courage and confidence, we can look to the future. If we don't look to the future, then where will we look? There are not many choices left. At least not a choice that leads to a more fulfilled and abundant life. Deep down inside, this is the kind of life we desire. We want to be more grateful. We want to feel and be more fulfilled. We sincerely wish for more abundance. Stephen King, author of many books said, "Get busy living or get busy dying." Sounds as if we are given a choice to make, once again. Life or death.

Truth be told it is only in working on living wholeheartedly every day that our lives will have true meaning. This is not a dress rehearsal. We must prepare now. This is our performance. Continue moving on until your journey's end. Look forward with confidence and keep expecting! You will marvel and be amazed at what you find waiting.

WHY I NEED TO LOOK TO THE FUTURE:

DO NOW: list as many reasons as come to your mind.

COMPLETE THIS SENTENCE:

Ways I can look to the future are…

I want to thank you sincerely from the bottom of my heart for going on this journey with me.

Hopefully, I have kept my promise to you that it was a great one! Along the way, I trust that you have picked up some helpful ideas that will enable you to live life to the fullest. My prayer is that you maintain your commitment to live now instead of waiting for tomorrow.

You have decided to change, to look at things differently, with "being grateful" eyes.

You took a chance and unlocked the door to a life of fulfillment and abundance. These "life-changing" attitudes have granted you your freedom. Congratulations!

With gratitude and much success,

Janice Almond

About the Author

As a first-time author, I am excited about the journey I am embarking on with readers like you from around the world.

Having been a pastor's wife, high school English teacher, community college professor, and involved in men's prison ministry, I have witnessed a myriad of human interactions that have positioned me to understand and communicate the behaviors that drive some toward success, and those that keep others in a slump.

I've had the privilege of traveling around Europe, joining Toastmasters, and receiving a B.A. degree in Communication Studies from UCLA during the John Wooden basketball years (1970's). Later, I earned two Master's degrees in Education, Multicultural Education and Educational Administration. Having spent more than a decade in education, it became my passion to share insights to better prepare students for life and to help them develop strong character. Now, it is my passion to share these lessons with the world.

My hope is that my works inspire, uplift, and encourage you to fulfill your full potential, and to live a life of purpose.

ONE LAST THING

Visit my website-
www.janicealmondbooks.com/contact

Sign up for my FREE monthly inspirational newsletter called, "Almond Joy" and as a bonus receive "The 7 Strategies to Get Focused"

email me:janicealmondbooks@gmail.com

NOTES

NOTES

NOTES

NOTES

NOTES

NOTES

NOTES

NOTES

NOTES

NOTES

www.ingramcontent.com/pod-product-compliance
Lightning Source LLC
Chambersburg PA
CBHW031452040426
42444CB00007B/1063